ACCOUNTING LIFEPA
PREPARING THE WORKS

CONTENTS

Author: Daniel L. Ritzman, B.S.

Editors: Alan Christopherson, M.S.

                  Jennifer L. Davis, B.S.

ALPHA OMEGA
PUBLICATIONS

300 North McKemy Avenue, Chandler, Arizona 85226-2618

ACCOUNTING LIFEPAC 5
PREPARING THE WORKSHEET

4 pgs. per day (handwritten)

OVERVIEW

Periodically the owner of a business needs to determine the financial results for the accounting period. That is, has the business income been greater than the business operating expenses? Has the business grown from one accounting cycle to the next? How do the income and expenses of this fiscal period compare to the previous period? Are the profits increasing, thus aiding in business expansion?

To answers these questions, reports must be prepared for the end of the fiscal period. The fifth step in the accounting cycle is to complete a worksheet. LIFEPAC 5 will show you how the worksheet is used to organize the information recorded in the general ledger accounts. You will also learn how to calculate the net income or net loss for the fiscal period.

OBJECTIVES

When you have completed this LIFEPAC you will be able to:

1. Define the accounting terms associated with the preparation of a worksheet;

2. Recognize accounting concepts and practices associated with a worksheet for a service business;

3. Explain why a business divides its accounting cycle into periods of equal length;

4. Understand and explain why a worksheet is prepared;

5. Describe the parts of a six-column worksheet;

6. Prepare a six-column worksheet;

7. Calculate net income and net loss using a six-column worksheet;

8. Describe the parts of an eight-column worksheet;

9. Plan the adjustments needed at the end of a fiscal period;

10. Explain why adjustments are needed for certain accounts;

11. Calculate net income and net loss using an eight-column worksheet; and

12. Find and correct common errors made in recording or calculating amounts.

Vocab (handwritten)

Study + learn

VOCABULARY

Adjustments – an adjustment is an amount that is added to or subtracted from an account balance to bring the balance up to date.

Balance Sheet – a financial statement that reports assets, liabilities and owner's equity on a specific date.

Consistent Reporting – the same accounting concepts are applied the same way for each accounting period for as long as the business operates.

Fiscal Period – the length of the accounting cycle for which a business summarizes and reports financial information.

Income Statement – a financial statement that reports the revenue and expenses for a fiscal period.

Matching Expenses with Revenue – all revenue and expenses associated with a business activity are to be recorded in the same accounting period.

Net – the amount remaining after all deductions have been made.

Net Income – the difference between total revenue and total expenses when total revenue is greater than total expenses.

Net Loss – the difference between total revenue and total expenses when total expenses are greater than total revenue.

Ruling – refers to drawing a line. A single line means the entries above are complete. A double line means the figures have been verified as correct.

Trial Balance – a proof of the equality of debits and credits in a general ledger.

Working Papers – informal, informational papers provided by accountants to owners and managers.

Worksheet – a columnar accounting form used to summarize the general ledger information needed to prepare financial statements.

SECTION I. PREPARING A SIX-COLUMN WORKSHEET

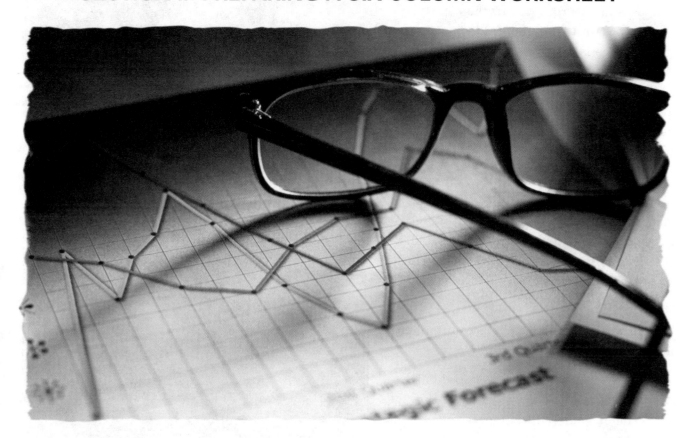

The general ledger accounts of any business contain vital information needed by managers and owners to determine the growth and profitability of that business. This information is presented account by account in the general ledger but is not very useful. In order for an owner or manager to interpret the information gathered, it must be analyzed, summarized and reported in an understandable and meaningful way. This is accomplished by applying the accounting concept of **consistent reporting**: the same accounting procedure is followed for each accounting period. The same methods of sorting, summarizing and analyzing business information are used for each accounting cycle.

The length of the accounting cycle for which a business summarizes and reports financial information is called a **fiscal period**. A company may choose any time period as a fiscal period—a month, a quarter, six months, or a year. The length of a fiscal period varies from one business to another. Each business can choose a fiscal period that will provide all the information it needs; however, since most federal and state reports are required annually, most businesses design an accounting period that corresponds with the state and federal tax reports. The most common fiscal period for most businesses is annual.

The accountant uses various methods of providing the owners and managers with information vital to all business decisions. The accountant organizes the data that is presented on the formal financial reports by preparing numerous informational reports in the form of memoranda, analysis papers and informal reports. These informal papers are often referred to as **working papers** and are an invaluable tool for accountants. One such tool is the **worksheet**. A worksheet is a columnar accounting form used to summarize the general ledger information needed to prepare the financial statements. This important working paper is not given to the owner or manger, however. It is prepared solely for the benefit of the accountant.

In LIFEPAC 4 you learned that all transactions are recorded in the general journal, posted to the general ledger and a trial balance is then prepared. If the trial balance is in balance, it proves the accuracy of the journalizing and posting process. For a small business, the trial balance is also used in the preparation of all formal financial reports.

However, if a company has a large number of accounts or has accounts that need to be adjusted to bring their balances up to date, the accountant takes the additional step of preparing a worksheet. This extra step decreases errors on the formal financial reports.

The worksheet helps the accountant to do the following:

1. Prepare the unadjusted trial balance to prove the equality of the debit and credit balances taken from the ledger;

2. Show the effects of the adjustments on the account balances to bring them up to date;

3. Sort the account balances into columns according to whether that account is used in preparing an income statement or a balance sheet; and

4. Calculate the amount of the net income or net loss for the fiscal period.

The preparation of the worksheet is the next step in the accounting cycle. The first four steps of the accounting cycle are performed frequently during the fiscal period. These steps include analyzing business transactions, journalizing transactions in the general journal, posting to the general ledger and preparing a trial balance.

Many business forms become part of the permanent records of a business. These records include source documents, journals and ledgers. Since these records are permanent, they are prepared in ink. However, the worksheet is not a permanent record of a business and is completed in pencil. Using pencil allows the accountant to correct errors easily, adjust accounts and extend balances without having to cross out amounts if mistakes are made.

The six-column worksheet is usually prepared by small sole proprietorship. These businesses are normally service-type businesses that do not accumulate a great number of assets or liabilities. Most of their income and expenses are easy to determine and calculate. The worksheet for such a business is prepared on standard, multi-column accounting paper. This columnar sheet may or may not include preprinted headings. Many accountants prefer the flexibility of entering their own column headings, while others prefer accounting papers with the heading already printed.

A six-column worksheet has five major parts, as illustrated below:

1. the heading,
2. the account number and account title section,
3. the trial balance section,
4. the income statement section, and
5. the balance sheet section.

ACCT NO.	2 ACCOUNT NAME	3 TRIAL BALANCE		4 INCOME STATEMENT		5 BALANCE SHEET	
		DEBIT	CREDIT	DEBIT	CREDIT	DEBIT	CREDIT

Where the top is labeled **1**.

The Heading Section

1	*Overview Tours*						
2	*Worksheet*						
3	*For the Month Ended July 31, 20—*						

ACCT NO.	ACCOUNT NAME	TRIAL BALANCE		INCOME STATEMENT		BALANCE SHEET	
		DEBIT	CREDIT	DEBIT	CREDIT	DEBIT	CREDIT

Just like the balance sheet and the trial balance, the heading on a worksheet consists of three lines that define *who*, *what* and *when*:

1. The name of the business   **WHO?**   "Overview Tours"
2. The name of the report   **WHAT?**   "Worksheet"
3. The date of the report   **WHEN?**   "For the Month ended July 31, 20__"

The above worksheet for Overview Tours has been prepared for the fiscal period ending July 31 of the current year and reflects the account balances for that accounting cycle.

The Account Title and Trial Balance Section

In LIFEPAC 4 you learned that a trial balance is prepared after completing a certain number of transactions. The trial balance provides proof of the equality of debits and credits in a general ledger and can be prepared at any time during a fiscal period. However, when a trial balance is prepared at the end of the accounting cycle, it is prepared on the trial balance section of the worksheet.

The general ledger provides the information needed to prepare the account title and trial balance sections of the worksheet. The account titles are listed on the worksheet in the same order as they appear in the general ledger—assets, liabilities, owner's equity, revenue and expenses. Accounts with normal debit balances will be listed in the debit column of the trial balance section of the worksheet. Accounts with normal credit balances are listed in the credit column of the trial balance section of the worksheet. Some accounts may have a zero balance. These accounts should also be listed to avoid omitting an account that appears in the general ledger. Listing all the accounts will insure that all information needed to prepare financial reports is available.

Steps for preparing the account title and the trial balance sections of the worksheet:

1. Write the general ledger account titles (and account numbers if a place is provided for them) in the account title section of the worksheet.

2. Copy the general ledger account *debit* balances to the trial balance debit column.

3. Copy the general ledger account *credit* balances to the trial balance credit column.

Overview Tours

Worksheet

For the Month Ended July 31, 20—

ACCT NO.	1 ACCOUNT NAME	TRIAL BALANCE 2 DEBIT	3 CREDIT	INCOME STATEMENT DEBIT	CREDIT	BALANCE SHEET DEBIT	CREDIT
110	Cash	24560 00					
120	Petty Cash	300 00					
130	Office Equipment	10000 00					
140	Garage Equipment	900 00					
210	Staples		450 00				
220	Town Supply		250 00				
310	John Jones, Capital		34850 00				
320	John Jones, Drawing	300 00					
410	Sales		1200 00				
510	Advertising Expense	50 00					
520	Miscellaneous Expense	150 00					
530	Rent Expense	450 00					
540	Utilities Expense	40 00					
5	Totals	36750 00	36750 00				

4. Rule a single line across the debit and credit columns after the last account entered. The single indicates that the columns are to be added. **Ruling** means drawing a line.

5. Write the word *Totals* below the single line and total both columns of the trial balance section. If the column totals are the same, then the debits and credits of the general ledger are in balance.

6. Rule a double line across the trial balance columns. This indicates the balances are equal and correct.

The Balance Sheet Section

As each fiscal period ends, two financial statements are prepared from the information gathered on the worksheet. These statements are used to answer the basic questions asked by the owner of every business: What is the owner's net worth (capital) and what is the net income (profit) for the fiscal period? **Net** refers to the amount that remains after all deductions have been made.

The **balance sheet** is the financial statement that answers the question about the owner's net worth or capital. A balance sheet lists the assets, the liabilities and the owner's equity (capital) for a specific date.

Overview Tours
Worksheet
For the Month Ended July 31, 20—

ACCT NO.	ACCOUNT NAME	TRIAL BALANCE DEBIT	TRIAL BALANCE CREDIT	INCOME STATEMENT DEBIT	INCOME STATEMENT CREDIT	BALANCE SHEET 1 DEBIT	BALANCE SHEET 2 CREDIT
110	Cash	24560 00				24560 00	
120	Petty Cash	300 00				300 00	
130	Office Equipment	10000 00				10000 00	
140	Garage Equipment	900 00				900 00	
210	Staples		450 00				450 00
220	Town Supply		250 00				250 00
310	John Jones, Capital		34850 00			3	34850 00
320	John Jones, Drawing	300 00				300 00	
410	Sales		1200 00				
510	Advertising Expense	50 00					
520	Miscellaneous Expense	150 00					
530	Rent Expense	450 00					
540	Utilities Expense	40 00					
	Totals	36750 00	36750 00				

The **income statement** is the financial statement that answers the question about net income. An income statement lists the revenue, expenses and the net income for a fiscal period. All up-to-date balances are extended to the proper columns of the worksheet for the two financial reports.

The balance sheet section of the worksheet contains the balances of the asset, liability and owner's equity accounts. The amounts are extended from the trial balance section. The accountant simply copies the balances of these accounts into the appropriate columns of the balance sheet section of the worksheet. These accounts are referred to as balance sheet accounts or real (permanent) accounts. These permanent accounts are carried from fiscal period to fiscal period for as long as the business exists.

The steps to extend balances to the balance sheet section are:

1. Extend the asset account debit balances.

2. Extend the liability account credit balances.

3. Extend the owner's equity account balances: the credit balance of the owner's capital account is extended to the credit column and the debit balance of the owner's drawing account is extended to the debit column of the balance sheet section.

The Income Statement Section

This section contains the balances of all revenue and expense accounts. Since revenue and expense accounts follow the assets, liabilities and owner's equity accounts on the trial balance, their balances are extended *after* completing the balance sheet section of the worksheet.

The steps for extending the revenue and expenses are as follows:

1. Extend the revenue account balance. Revenue accounts have a credit balance; therefore, they are extended to the credit column of the income statement section of the worksheet.

2. Extend the balances of all expenses. Expense accounts have debit balances; therefore, they are extended to the debit column of the income statement section of the worksheet.

Overview Tours

Worksheet

For the Month Ended July 31, 20—

ACCT NO.	ACCOUNT NAME	TRIAL BALANCE DEBIT	TRIAL BALANCE CREDIT	INCOME STATEMENT DEBIT	INCOME STATEMENT CREDIT	BALANCE SHEET DEBIT	BALANCE SHEET CREDIT
110	Cash	24560 00					
120	Petty Cash	300 00					
130	Office Equipment	10000 00					
140	Garage Equipment	900 00					
210	Staples		450 00				
220	Town Supply		250 00				
310	John Jones, Capital		34850 00				
320	John Jones, Drawing	300 00					
410	Sales		1200 00		**1** 1200 00		
510	Advertising Expense	50 00		**2** 50 00			
520	Miscellaneous Expense	150 00		150 00			
530	Rent Expense	450 00		450 00			
540	Utilities Expense	40 00		40 00			
	Totals	36750 00	36750 00				

ACCT NO.	ACCOUNT NAME	TRIAL BALANCE		INCOME STATEMENT		BALANCE SHEET	
		DEBIT	CREDIT	DEBIT	CREDIT	DEBIT	CREDIT
110	Cash	24560 00				24560 00	
120	Petty Cash	300 00				300 00	
130	Office Equipment	10000 00				10000 00	
140	Garage Equipment	900 00				900 00	
210	Staples		450 00				450 00
220	Town Supply		250 00				250 00
310	John Jones, Capital		34850 00				34850 00
320	John Jones, Drawing	300 00				300 00	
410	Sales		1200 00		1200 00		
510	Advertising Expense	50 00		50 00			
520	Miscellaneous Expense	150 00		150 00			
530	Rent Expense	450 00		450 00			
540	Utilities Expense	40 00		40 00			
	Totals	36750 00	36750 00	690 00	1200 00	36060 00	35550 00

Difference: $510.00   Difference: $510.00

After extending the amounts in the trial balance section to the income statement and balance sheet section, the columns are then totaled as shown above. A single line is drawn across the last four columns to indicate they are to be added. Unlike the trial balance section of the worksheet, in these two sections the *debits and credits do not equal*. The difference between the column totals ($510.00) represents the net income or net loss for the fiscal period.

Calculating Net Income

The **net income** is the difference between total revenue and total expenses when total revenue is greater than total expenses. A **net loss** would occur when the total expenses were greater than the total revenue for a fiscal period.

Revenue for a fiscal period is always matched with expenses for the same period. The income statement section includes both the revenue and expenses for the fiscal period. After the columns have been totaled, the total expenses (the debit column total) are subtracted from total revenue (the credit column total) to find the net income.

The net income must also be transferred to the balance sheet section of the worksheet. Revenue and expense accounts are temporary *capital* accounts. At the end of the fiscal period, the net income is transferred to the capital account in the ledger by using an account called *Income*

ACCT NO.	ACCOUNT NAME	TRIAL BALANCE		INCOME STATEMENT		BALANCE SHEET	
		DEBIT	CREDIT	DEBIT	CREDIT	DEBIT	CREDIT
110	Cash	24560 00				24560 00	
120	Petty Cash	300 00				300 00	
130	Office Equipment	10000 00				10000 00	
140	Garage Equipment	900 00				900 00	
210	Staples		450 00				450 00
220	Town Supply		250 00				250 00
310	John Jones, Capital		34850 00				34850 00
320	John Jones, Drawing	300 00				300 00	
410	Sales		1200 00		1200 00		
510	Advertising Expense	50 00		50 00			
520	Miscellaneous Expense	150 00		150 00			
530	Rent Expense	450 00		450 00			
540	Utilities Expense	40 00		1 40 00			
	Totals	36750 00	36750 00	2 690 00	1200 00	36060 00	35550 00
3	Net Income			4 510 00			510 00
				5 1200 00	1200 00	36060 00	36060 00

Summary. The Income Summary account will be explained in detail in LIFEPAC 7. Since the capital account is increased by a credit, the amount of the net income is added to the total of the balance sheet credit column on the worksheet, as illustrated above:

1. Rule a single line across the four columns of the income statement and balance sheet sections of the worksheet.

2. Add both debit and credit columns of the income statement and balance sheet sections. Write the total below the single line. Net income is the difference between the debit and credit columns of the income statement section of the worksheet.

3. Write the amount of net income below the income statement debit column total. Write the words *Net Income* on the same line in the account title column.

4. Since the owner's capital account is increased by the net income of the business, Capital must be credited to increase its value. Extend the amount of net income to the balance sheet *credit* column on the same line as the words *Net Income*.

5. Draw a single line underneath the net income amounts and bring down the totals of these four columns. Check the equality of the debits and credits in the columns and draw a double rule underneath to indicate that the totals are correct and the form is complete.

Complete the following activity.

The account balances for the **Fox Amusement Park** for the fiscal period ending October 31 of the current year are given below.

Account No. & Title		Debit	Credit
110	Cash	$ 4,580.00	
120	Concession Equipment	5,800.00	
130	Repair Equipment	7,800.00	
210	Concession Supply Co.		$ 1,560.00
310	Jason Fox, Capital		10,200.00
320	Jason Fox, Drawing	900.00	
410	Admissions Income		11,500.00
420	Concessions Income		2,600.00
510	Advertising Expense	2,500.00	
520	Rent Expense	3,500.00	
530	Utilities Expense	780.00	

1.1   Using the above information, prepare a worksheet for the **Fox Amusement Park** for the month ended October 31 of the current year.

Instructions:

1. **Write the heading** on the worksheet.
2. **List all of the account numbers, titles and balances** in the trial balance section.
3. **Balance and rule** the trial balance.
4. **Extend the amounts** of the trial balance section to the balance sheet and income statement sections.
5. **Total the columns** for the income statement and balance sheet sections.
6. **Calculate** the Net Income or Net Loss.
7. **Enter the amount of Net Income or Net Loss** in the proper column of the balance sheet and income statement sections.
8. **Total and rule** the income statement and balance sheet sections.

Blue

Worksheet for Exercise 1.1

Aubrey Elizabeth B.O

Fox Amusement Park
Worksheet
For the month ended October 31, 2008

ACCT NO.	ACCOUNT NAME	TRIAL BALANCE		INCOME STATEMENT		BALANCE SHEET	
		DEBIT	CREDIT	DEBIT	CREDIT	DEBIT	CREDIT
110	Cash	4,580 00				4,580 00	
130	Concession Equipment	5,800 00				5,800 00	
130	Repair Equipment	7,800 00				7,800 00	
310	Concession Supply Co.		1560 00				1560 00
310	Jason Fox Capital		10,200 00				10,200 00
330	Jason Fox Drawing	900 00				900 00	
410	Admission Income		11,500 00		11,500 00		
420	Concession Income		2,000 00		2,000 00		
510	Advertising Expense	2500 00		2500 00			
500	Rent Expense	3500 00		3500 00			
530	Utilities Expense	780 00		780 00			
	Total	25,860 00	25,860 00	6,780 00	14,100 00	19,080 00	11,760 00
	Net Income			7,320 00			7,320 00
				14,100 00	14,100 00	19,080 00	19,080 00

Complete the following activity.

The account balances for **Johnson's Computer Services** for the fiscal period ending December 31 of the current year are given below.

Account No. & Title		Debit	Credit
110	Cash	$ 2,580.00	
120	Computer Supplies	800.00	
130	Delivery Equipment	10,600.00	
140	Repair Equipment	7,800.00	
210	Computer Supply Co.		$ 6,560.00
310	Kellie Johnson, Capital		19,200.00
320	Kellie Johnson, Drawing	1,900.00	
410	Computer Sales		11,500.00
420	Repair Income		11,500.00
510	Advertising Expense	12,500.00	
520	Miscellaneous Expense	1,200.00	
530	Rent Expense	9,600.00	
540	Utilities Expense	1,780.00	

1.2   Using the above information, prepare a worksheet for the **Johnson's Computer Service** for the month ended December 31 of the current year.

Instructions:

1. **Write the heading** on the worksheet.
2. **List all of the account numbers, titles and balances** in the trial balance section.
3. **Balance and rule** the trial balance.
4. **Extend the amounts** of the trial balance section to the balance sheet and income statement sections.

5. **Total the columns** for the income statement and balance sheet sections.
6. **Calculate** the Net Income or Net Loss.
7. **Enter the amount of Net Income or Net Loss** in the proper column of the balance sheet and income statement sections.
8. **Total and rule** the income statement and balance sheet sections.

Johnson's Computer Services
Worksheet
For the month ended December 31, 2003

ACCT NO.	ACCOUNT NAME	TRIAL BALANCE		INCOME STATEMENT		BALANCE SHEET	
		DEBIT	CREDIT	DEBIT	CREDIT	DEBIT	CREDIT
110	Cash	2580 00				2580 00	
120	Computer Supplies	800 00				800 00	
130	Delivery Equipment	10,400 00				10,400 00	
140	Repair Equipment	7,800 00				7,800 00	
210	Computer Supply Co.		6,560 00				6560 00
310	Kellie Johnson, Capital		19,200 00				19,200 00
320	Kellie Johnson, Drawing	1900 00				1900 00	
410	Computer Sales		11,500 00		11,500 00		
420	Repair Income		11,500 00		11,500 00		
610	Advertising Expense	12,500 00		12,500 00			
520	Miscellaneous Expense	1,200 00		1,200 00			
530	Rent Expense	9,600 00		9,600 00			
540	Utilities Expense	1,780 00		1,780 00			
	Total	48,760 00	48,760 00	25,080 00	23,000 00	23,080 00	25,760 00
	Net Income			2,080 00			2,080 00
				25,080 00	25,080 00	25,760 00	25,760 00

Complete the following activity.

The account balances for **Lawson's Travel Agency** for the fiscal period ending June 30 of the current year are given below.

Account No. & Title		Debit	Credit
110	Cash	$ 9,450.00	
120	Accounts Receivable	4,860.00	
130	Office Equipment	17,800.00	
140	Office Supplies	800.00	
150	Furniture	1,600.00	
210	Accounts Payable		$ 6,890.00
220	Sales Tax Payable		950.00
310	Donald Lawson, Capital		26,390.00
320	Donald Lawson, Drawing	900.00	
410	Fees Income		10,550.00
510	Entertainment Expense	290.00	
520	Miscellaneous Expense	200.00	
530	Rent Expense	600.00	
540	Travel Expense	6,500.00	
550	Utilities Expense	1,780.00	

1.3 Using the above information, prepare a worksheet for **Lawson's Travel Agency** for the month ended June 30 of the current year.

Instructions:

1. **Write the heading** on the worksheet.
2. **List all of the account numbers, titles and balances** in the trial balance section.
3. **Balance and rule** the trial balance.
4. **Extend the amounts** of the trial balance section to the balance sheet and income statement sections.
5. **Total the columns** for the income statement and balance sheet sections.
6. **Calculate** the Net Income or Net Loss.
7. **Enter the amount of Net Income or Net Loss** in the proper column of the balance sheet and income statement sections.
8. **Total and rule** the income statement and balance sheet sections.

Worksheet for Exercise 1.3

Lawson's Travel Agency
Worksheet
For the month ended June 30, 2003

ACCT NO.	ACCOUNT NAME	TRIAL BALANCE DEBIT	TRIAL BALANCE CREDIT	INCOME STATEMENT DEBIT	INCOME STATEMENT CREDIT	BALANCE SHEET DEBIT	BALANCE SHEET CREDIT
110	Cash	9450 00				9450 00	
120	Accounts Receivable	4,860 00				4,860 00	
130	Office Equipment	17,800 00				17,800 00	
140	Office Supplies	800 00				800 00	
150	Furniture	1600 00				1600 00	
210	Accounts Payable		6890 00				6890 00
220	Sales Tax Payable		950 00				
310	Donald Lawson, Capital		26,390 00				26,390 00
330	Donald Lawson, Drawing	900 00				900 00	
410	Fees Income		10,550 00		10,550 00		
510	Entertainment Expense	290 00		290 00			
520	Miscellaneous Expense	200 00		200 00			
530	Rent Expense	600 00		600 00			
540	Travel Expense	6,500 00		6,500 00			
550	Utilities Expense	1,780 00		1,780 00			
	Total	44,780 00	44,780 00	9370 00	10,550 00	35,410 00	33,280 00
	Net Income			1180 00			2130 00
				10,550 00	10,550 00	35,410 00	35,410 00

Review the material in this section in preparation for the Self Test. The Self Test will check your mastery of this particular section. The items missed on this Self Test will indicate specific areas where restudy is needed for mastery.

SELF TEST 1

94% Quiz

Complete the following activities (each answer, 4 points).

1.01 What is a fiscal period? _Is the length of an accounting cycle in which a business summarizes & reports finiancal information_

1.02 What is the normal length of a fiscal period and why? _annually. most business like to go with the state & federal tax reports which are annual._

1.03 List other possible fiscal periods. _monthly, quarterly, every six months, or yearly_

1.04 List four reasons for preparing a worksheet.

taken from the general ledger

a. _Prepare an adjustment Trail balance To prove the equality of THe Debit & credit balance_

b. _Show the effect of the adjustments on the account balances to bring them up to DATe_ _or balance sheets_

c. _Sort the accounts into columns to determine if They will be used For income statement_

d. _Caculate the Net income or Net loss in THe capital_

1.05 Why is it permissible to prepare a worksheet in pencil? _Because the worksheet is not a perminate record. So it's easy To eras, mistakes & corect them instead of crossing them out._

1.06 List the five parts of a six-column worksheet.

a. _HEADING_

b. _Account Titles_

c. _TRAIl BAlANCE_

d. _iNCOME STATEMENT_

e. _BAlANCE SHEET_

1.07 What three items appear in the heading of the worksheet?

a. _Name of business or company_ _who_

b. _What kind of Financial STATEMENT_ _what_

c. _The time period when The statement was being recorded_ _when_ _FINANcial_

1.08 How are the accounts listed in the account title section? _____

According to the general ledger — a, l, c, r & e

1.09 What controls the order of the accounts in the general ledger? _____

The chart of accounts = which orders them by account numbers & account titles

1.010 What effect does net income have on the owner's capital account? _____

Net income increases the owner's capital

1.011 How is net income shown on the balance sheet section of a worksheet? *as a credit entry*

When the assets & capital are more than the liabilities

1.012 What is the purpose of a single line ruled under a column of numbers on the worksheet?

A single line indicates the # above are complete & ready to be

added.

1.013 What is the effect of a net loss on the owner's capital account? _____

A decrease in the owner's capital or (equity)

1.014 How is a net loss shown on the balance sheet section of a worksheet? *(as a debit entry)*

When liability is more than the asset & capital put together

1.015 What is the purpose of a double line drawn across two columns of a worksheet? _____

Tells you that everything is complete, correct & in balance

1.016 After completing the trial balance section of a worksheet, to which section do you extend the balances of assets, liabilities and owner's equity? _____

Balance sheet column

1.017 After completing the trial balance section of a worksheet, to which section do you extend the balances of revenue and expenses? _____

To the income/statement column

Cash	1.00	
Pre Insur	2.00	
Office Equp	1.00	
Office Depou		2.00
Neds Capital		3.00

83/104

Score ___94___

Adult Check ___SB___

Initial   Date

19

SECTION II. PREPARING AN EIGHT-COLUMN WORKSHEET

The eight-column worksheet is prepared by a majority of businesses such as service, merchandising and manufacturing businesses that accumulate a great number of assets or liabilities. This type of worksheet is used by all forms of business organizations—both profit and non-profit.

An eight-column worksheet has six major parts that are illustrated on the worksheet shown below:

1. the heading,
2. the account title section,
3. the trial balance section,
4. the adjustments section,
5. the income statement section, and
6. the balance sheet section.

1								
2	3		4		5		6	
ACCOUNT TITLE	TRIAL BALANCE		ADJUSTMENTS		INCOME STATEMENT		BALANCE SHEET	
	DEBIT	CREDIT	DEBIT	CREDIT	DEBIT	CREDIT	DEBIT	CREDIT

The Heading Section

Like the heading on a six-column worksheet, the eight-column worksheet heading consists of three lines: **WHO** (the name of the business), **WHAT** (the name of the report) and **WHEN** (the date of the report).

Lawson's Lawn Care
Worksheet
For the Month Ended July 31, 20—

ACCOUNT TITLE	TRIAL BALANCE		ADJUSTMENTS		INCOME STATEMENT		BALANCE SHEET	
	DEBIT	CREDIT	DEBIT	CREDIT	DEBIT	CREDIT	DEBIT	CREDIT
Cash	7822 00							
Petty Cash	300 00							
Supplies	4319 00							
Prepaid Insurance	1600 00							
John's Garage		1630 00						
Wick Supplies		300 00						
D. Lawson, Capital		9000 00						
D. Lawson, Drawing	500 00							
Sales		4367 00						
Advertising Expense	86 00							
Insurance Expense								
Miscellaneous Expense	95 00							
Rent Expense	450 00							
Supplies Expense								
Utilities Expense	125 00							
Totals	15297 00	15297 00						

The Account Title and Trial Balance Section

This section of the worksheet is prepared in the same manner as the six-column worksheet. Every account, even if it has a zero balance, is listed in the trial balance section of the worksheet in the same order in which it appears in the general ledger: assets first, liabilities second, owner's equity third, revenue fourth and expenses fifth.

Enter the account balances as they appear in the general ledger accounts, being careful to list accounts with debit balances in the "Debit" column and accounts with credit balances in the "Credit" column.

After transferring the ledger account balances, rule and total the debit and credit columns. If the columns are the same, draw a double line under the totals in the trial balance columns. This indicates the balances are equal and correct.

Planning Adjustments on a Worksheet

Many owners and managers assume that the only changes that affect account balances result from daily business transactions. However, some account balances change due to the daily internal operations of the business.

For example, a business will pay cash for supplies during one fiscal period, but the supplies are not used up until a future fiscal period. Some supplies purchased during this fiscal period will be left over and consumed during the next accounting cycle.

Another example is prepaid insurance. Insurance is usually paid for a year in advance. During a monthly fiscal period, the unexpired insurance must be carried over as an asset for the next accounting cycle. The expired insurance becomes an expense for this fiscal period. The Insurance Expense account reflects the actual amount of insurance "consumed" during the fiscal period.

It is important that a business match the expenses of a fiscal period with the revenue it produced during the fiscal period. By matching revenue with expenses, a more accurate indication of business performance is obtained than by comparing cash receipts and cash payments for the same period. The accounting concept of **matching expenses with revenue** states that all revenue and expenses associated with a business activity are to be recorded in the same accounting period.

The cost of the goods and services used in the operation of a business are expenses. Normally, items bought for business use are recorded as assets. As the business consumes these assets, they become expenses of the business. They are expended in the sense that as the assets are consumed, they become the expense of doing business. At the end of the fiscal period, therefore, **adjustments** must be made to transfer these costs to the proper expense account. Adjustments must also be made before the correct net income or net loss can be determined.

As you have learned in previous LIFEPACs, account balances were only changed through journal entries that were then posted to each individual account. The source document was the evidence needed to make such journal entries. Since changes caused by internal business operations *do not* produce a source document, these changes must be shown at the end of a fiscal period by adjusting the account balance. An **adjustment** is an amount that is added to or subtracted from an account balance to bring the balance up to date.

Since some of the accounts shown in the trial balance section of the worksheet are not up to date, these accounts must be adjusted. Each adjustment made will affect one permanent (real) account and one temporary account.

The adjustments section of the worksheet is used to calculate the amounts necessary to bring these accounts up to date. The bookkeeper does not change any accounts in the general ledger until the accuracy of each adjustment is checked on the worksheet and the financial reports are prepared. Then, and only then, will the adjustments be journalized and posted.

Lawson's Lawn Care
Worksheet
For the Month Ended July 31, 20—

ACCOUNT TITLE	TRIAL BALANCE		ADJUSTMENTS		INCOME STATEMENT		BALANCE SHEET	
	DEBIT	CREDIT	DEBIT	CREDIT	DEBIT	CREDIT	DEBIT	CREDIT
Cash	7822 00							
Petty Cash	300 00							
Supplies	4319 00							
Prepaid Insurance	1600 00							
John's Garage		1630 00						
Wick Supplies		300 00						
D. Lawson, Capital		9000 00						
D. Lawson, Drawing	500 00							
Sales		4367 00						
Advertising Expense	86 00							
Insurance Expense								
Miscellaneous Expense	95 00							
Rent Expense	450 00							
Supplies Expense								
Utilities Expense	125 00							
Totals	15297 00	15297 00						

Adjusting Supplies for Lawson's Lawn Care. Throughout the accounting cycle, Lawson's Lawn Care has been purchasing and consuming supplies during daily business operations. However, the balance in the general ledger reflects only the supplies purchased. This balance was transferred to the trial balance section of the worksheet. At the end of the fiscal period, an actual count of supplies on hand must be made to determine the value of supplies consumed (expended) during the accounting cycle, and the Supplies account must be adjusted to reflect the current value of the supplies still on hand.

Two accounts are affected by this adjustment—one permanent account (Supplies) and one temporary account (Supplies Expense).

General Ledger Balances Before Adjustment. Shown below are what the general ledger accounts look like before the adjustment to Supplies is made.

Account Title: *Supplies*						Account No. *130*	
Date 20—	**Explanation**	**Post. Ref.**	**Debit**	**Credit**	**Balance**	
					Debit	**Credit**
July 31					4319 00	

Account Title: *Supplies Expense*						Account No. *550*	
Date 20—	**Explanation**	**Post. Ref.**	**Debit**	**Credit**	**Balance**	
					Debit	**Credit**

At the end of the fiscal period, Mr. Lawson counted the supplies on hand and it was determined that the value of the supplies inventory was $2,978.00. The value of the Supplies asset account was calculated as follows:

Supplies Account Balance, July 31	$4,319.00
Supplies Inventory, July 31	2,978.00
Supplies Used During July	$1,341.00

Analyzing the Adjustment Transaction. The amount of $1,341.00 represents the value of the supplies expended or used during the month of July. The temporary Supplies Expense account needs to be increased and the permanent Supplies asset account needs to be decreased.

As stated previously, the general ledger accounts are not changed until the accuracy of each adjustment is checked on the worksheet. Then, and only then, will the adjustments be journalized and posted.

Accounts Affected	Classification of Each Account	Changes in Account Balance	How Change is Entered
Supplies Expense	Expense	Increase	Debit
Supplies	Asset	Decrease	Credit

Recording the Supplies Adjustment on the Worksheet.

1. Enter the debit of $1,341.00 to Supplies Expense in the adjustment debit column.
2. Enter the credit to Supplies in the adjustment credit column.
3. Enter (a) to label each adjustment. The letter indicates the debit and credit part of the same adjustment.

Lawson's Lawn Care

Worksheet

For the Month Ended July 31, 20—

ACCOUNT TITLE	TRIAL BALANCE		ADJUSTMENTS		INCOME STATEMENT		BALANCE SHEET	
	DEBIT	CREDIT	DEBIT	CREDIT	DEBIT	CREDIT	DEBIT	CREDIT
Cash	7822 00							
Petty Cash	300 00							
Supplies	4319 00			(a)1341 00				
Prepaid Insurance	1600 00			(b)330 00				
John's Garage		1630 00						
Wick Supplies		300 00						
D. Lawson, Capital		9000 00						
D. Lawson, Drawing	500 00							
Sales		4367 00						
Advertising Expense	86 00							
Insurance Expense			(b)330 00					
Miscellaneous Expense	95 00							
Rent Expense	450 00							
Supplies Expense			(a)1341 00					
Utilities Expense	125 00							
Totals	15297 00	15297 00	1671 00	1671 00				

Adjusting Prepaid Insurance for Lawson's Lawn Care. Lawson's Lawn Care purchased an insurance policy covering several fiscal periods. To record the insurance expense during daily business operations would be time-consuming, and errors could easily be made. Therefore, it is necessary to determine the expired insurance at the end of the fiscal period and make an adjusting entry. The asset Prepaid Insurance will contain the amount of the unexpired insurance, and the Insurance Expense account will contain the amount of insurance that expired during the accounting period.

General Ledger Balances Before Adjustment. Shown on the next page are what the general ledger accounts look like before the adjustment to Prepaid Insurance is made.

Account Title: *Prepaid Insurance*					Account No. *140*		
Date 20—	Explanation	Post. Ref.	Debit	Credit	Balance		
					Debit	Credit	
July 31					1600 00		

Account Title: *Insurance Expense*					Account No. *520*		
Date 20—	Explanation	Post. Ref.	Debit	Credit	Balance		
					Debit	Credit	

At the end of the fiscal period, Mr. Lawson verified that the value of Prepaid Insurance should be $1,270.00. The value of this asset account at the end of the fiscal period was calculated as follows:

Prepaid Insurance Account Balance, July 31	$1,600.00
Unexpired Insurance as of July 31	1,270.00
Insurance Expense During July	$330.00

Analyzing the Adjustment Transaction. The amount of $330.00 represents the value of the insurance expended or used during the month of July. The temporary account (Insurance Expense) needs to be increased and the permanent asset account (Prepaid Insurance) needs to be decreased.

Accounts Affected	Classification of Each Account	Changes in Account Balance	How Change is Entered
Insurance Expense	Expense	Increase	Debit
Prepaid Insurance	Decrease	Decrease	Credit

Recording the Prepaid Insurance Adjustment on the Worksheet. The adjustment to the Prepaid Insurance account is made on the worksheet on the previous page.

4. Enter the debit of $330.00 to Insurance Expense in the adjustments debit column.

5. Enter the credit to Prepaid Insurance in the adjustments credit column.

6. Enter (b) to label each adjustment. The letter indicates the debit and credit part of the same adjustment.

Totaling and Ruling the Adjustment Columns on the Worksheet.

7. Extend the single line from the trial balance columns across the adjustments columns.

8. Add the debit and credit adjustments columns. If the totals are the same, the adjustments section is in balance.

9. Double rule across the adjustment columns to indicate the totals are correct.

ACCOUNTING

LIFEPAC TEST

90 / 113

Name _Aubrey Bird_

Date _____

Score _97_

LIFEPAC TEST ACCOUNTING 5

PART I

On the blank, print a *T* if the statement is true or an *F* if the statement is false (each correct answer, 1 point).

1. __F__ If an error occurs during the accounting process, an adjusting entry must be made.

2. __T__ The consumed portion of some business assets becomes business expenses during the accounting period.

3. __F__ When analyzing an adjustment, *Who*, *What* and *When* are the important questions to ask.

4. __T__ The report date is written on the third line of the heading on a worksheet.

5. __T__ The worksheet summarizes financial information used to prepare a business's financial statements.

6. __F__ At the end of a fiscal period, an expense account will have a credit balance.

7. __F__ A net loss occurs when total revenue for the fiscal period exceeds the total expenses for the same period.

8. __T__ A net income occurs when total revenue for the fiscal period exceeds the total expenses for the same period.

9. __T__ If the Cash account balance is found on the trial balance debit column, it is transferred to the balance sheet debit column.

10. __F__ The debit entry in the adjustments column for Supplies Expense represents the amount of supplies purchased during the fiscal period.

11. __T__ Adjustments are made to certain asset accounts at the end of a fiscal period to bring their balances up to date.

12. __F__ The balance sheet columns of a worksheet contain the balances of revenue and expense account of the business.

13. __T__ To adjust an asset, it is important to know the amount used during a fiscal period.

14. __T__ The value of certain assets is determined by the inventory on hand at the end of a fiscal period.

15. __T__ The adjustment to Insurance Expense represents the expired insurance for the fiscal period.

16. __T__ The accounts affected by the adjustment to supplies are Supplies and Supplies Expense.

17. __T__ The income statement sections of the worksheet contains the revenue and expense account balances.

18. __F__ The accounts affected by the adjustment to prepaid insurance are Insurance Expense and Cash.

1

19. _T_ The credit to Prepaid Insurance in the adjustments column of the worksheet represents the expired insurance for the fiscal period.

20. _T_ The debit balance to Supplies in the balance sheet debit column represents the Supplies on hand at the end of a fiscal period.

21. _T_ The balances of any liability in the trial balance credit column are copied to the balance sheet credit column.

22. _T_ If the business shows a net income, the income statement credit column will be larger than the income statement debit column.

23. _F_ If the balance sheet debit column is smaller than the balance sheet credit column, the business shows a net income.

24. _F_ Revenue is the cost of goods and services used in the operation of a business.

25. _F_ The Cash account balance is never adjusted at the end of a fiscal period.

For each statement below, circle the letter of the choice that best completes the sentence (each answer, 1 point).

26. The second line on the heading of a worksheet is:
   a. the name of the report
   b. the name of the business
   c. the current fiscal period
   d. the current date

27. The expenses of a business are found in the worksheet's:
   a. adjustments columns,
   b. income statement columns
   c. balance sheet columns
   d. none of the above

28. If the difference between the trial balance debit column total and the trial balance credit column total is $9.00, the error most likely is:
   a. in addition
   b. in posting
   c. a transposition or slide
   d. in copying from the general ledger

29. The accounts in the account title section of a worksheet are listed:
   a. alphabetically
   b. numerically
   c. as listed in the general ledger
   d. random order

2

30. The fiscal period of a business represents:
    a. the length of the accounting cycle
    b. a calendar year
    c. an accounting year
    d. a revenue cycle

31. While proving the totals of the balance sheet section of the worksheet, a $100.00 difference between the columns was discovered. This type of error is most likely caused by:
    a. posting
    b. addition
    c. a slide
    d. subtraction

32. When preparing a worksheet and financial statements, the accountant is applying the accounting concept of:
    a. matching revenue and expenses
    b. accounting period cycle
    c. consistent reporting
    d. realization of revenue

33. What is the purpose of a single line ruled under a column of numbers on a worksheet?
    a. indicates the last number has been entered
    b. indicates the end of a financial statement
    c. indicates the last number is subtracted from the total
    d. signifies the column is complete and ready to be added

34. How does a net income from business operations affect the owner's capital account?
    a. has no effect on the owner's capital account
    b. increases the value of the owner's capital account
    c. decreases the value of the owner's capital account
    d. none of the above

35. When a double line is drawn across two columns of a worksheet, this signifies that the column totals are:
    a. correct and complete
    b. to be transferred to the next column
    c. are incorrect
    d. are not complete

36. Which of the following errors would not show up on the trial balance section of a worksheet?
    a. addition error
    b. a slide
    c. a transaction never recorded
    d. copying a balance incorrectly

3

37. If an account has a debit balance, it is because:
    a. all general ledger accounts have debit balances
    b. the business shows a net income
    c. the business has no debits
    d. the account's debits are larger than the account's credits

38. Of the following accounts, locate the one affected by an adjusting entry:
    a. Cash
    b. Prepaid Insurance
    c. Rent Expense
    d. Equipment

39. How does a net loss affect the balance of the owner's capital account?
    a. increases the balance
    b. has no effect on the balance
    c. decreases the balance
    d. transfers the balance to the cash account

40. The business form used to summarize the financial condition of a business on a specific date is:
    a. an income statement
    b. a balance sheet
    c. an owner's equity statement
    d. a worksheet

CORRECT complete in balance

Part II

On April 30th of the current year, the **Craft Shop** has the following general ledger accounts and balances. The business has a monthly fiscal period.

Account Titles	Debit	Credit
Cash	12,454.00	
Petty Cash	300.00	
Supplies – Office	2,950.00	
Prepaid Insurance	3,800.00	
Jones Office Supply		1,771.00
Craft Supply, Inc.		1,660.00
Jane Smith, Capital		13,099.00
Jane Smith, Drawing	1,560.00	
Sales		8,834.00
Advertising Expense	1,775.00	
Insurance Expense		
Miscellaneous Expense	615.00	
Rent Expense	1,000.00	
Repair Expense	885.00	
Supplies Expense – Office		
Utilities Expense	25.00	

Instructions:

41.
  a. Prepare the heading on the worksheet.

  b. Prepare the trial balance. Enter account titles and balances.

  c. Total and rule the trial balance columns.

  d. Analyze the following adjustment information into debit and credit parts. Record the adjustments on the worksheet adjustments columns.

  Office Supplies on hand: $1,101.00

  Value of Prepaid Insurance: $2,400.00

  e. Total and rule the adjustments columns.

  f. Extend the updated balances to the balance sheet columns.

  g. Extend the updated balances to the income statement columns.

  h. Rule a single line across the income statement and balance sheet columns. Total the columns. Calculate the net income or net loss. Label the amount properly in the account title column.

  i. Total and rule the income statement and balance sheet columns.

5

Worksheet for Exercise 41

Craft Shop
Worksheet
For the month ended April 30, 2003

ACCOUNT NAME	TRIAL BALANCE DEBIT	TRIAL BALANCE CREDIT	ADJUSTMENTS DEBIT	ADJUSTMENTS CREDIT	INCOME STATEMENT DEBIT	INCOME STATEMENT CREDIT	BALANCE SHEET DEBIT	BALANCE SHEET CREDIT
Cash	12,454 00						12,454 00	
Petty Cash	300 00						300 00	
Supplies - Office	2,950 00			(a) 1849 00			1,101 00	
Prepaid Insurance	3,800 00			(b) 1400 00			2,400 00	
Jane Office Supply		1771 00						1771 00
Craft Supply, Inc.		1,660 00						1,660 00
Jane Smith, Capital		13,099 00						13,099 00
Jane Smith, Drawing	1560 00						1560 00	
Sales		8,834 00				8834 00		
Advertising Expense	1775 00				1775 00			
Insurance Expense			(b) 1400 00		1400 00			
Miscellaneous Expense	615 00				615 00			
Rent Expense	1000 00				1000 00			
Repair Expense	885 00				885 00			
Supplies Expense - Office			(a) 1849 00		1849 00			
Utilities Expense	25 00				25 00			
Total	25,364 00	25,364 00	3,249 00	3,249 00	7549 00	8834 00	17815 00	16,530 00
Net income					1385 00			1385 00
					8834 00	8834 00	17815 00	17815 00

6

NOTES

Lawson's Lawn Care
Worksheet
For the Month Ended July 31, 20—

ACCOUNT TITLE	TRIAL BALANCE DEBIT	TRIAL BALANCE CREDIT	ADJUSTMENTS DEBIT	ADJUSTMENTS CREDIT	INCOME STATEMENT DEBIT	INCOME STATEMENT CREDIT		BALANCE SHEET DEBIT	BALANCE SHEET CREDIT
Cash	7822 00							7822 00	
Petty Cash	300 00						1	300 00	
Supplies	4319 00			(a)1341 00				2978 00	
Prepaid Insurance	1600 00			(b) 330 00				1270 00	
John's Garage		1630 00							1630 00
Wick Supplies		300 00					2		300 00
D. Lawson, Capital		9000 00							9000 00
D. Lawson, Drawing	500 00						3	500 00	
Sales		4367 00							
Advertising Expense	86 00								
Insurance Expense			(b) 330 00						
Miscellaneous Expense	95 00								
Rent Expense	450 00								
Supplies Expense			(a)1341 00						
Utilities Expense	125 00								
Totals	15297 00	15297 00	1671 00	1671 00					

Extending Balance Sheet Accounts on the Worksheet

Just like the six-column worksheet you completed earlier in this LIFEPAC, the balance sheet section of the eight-column worksheet contains the balances of the asset, liabilities and owner's equity accounts. The amounts are extended from the trial balance section. The accountant simply copies the balances of these accounts into the appropriate columns of the balance sheet section of the worksheet, checking for adjustments that might have been made to bring the accounts up to date.

1. **Extend the asset account balances.** Debit balances for all assets are extended to the debit column of the balance sheet section. Verify that they are up to date by checking for figures in the adjustments section of the worksheet.

   ✗ The Cash and Petty Cash account balances are up to date because there are no adjustments to change the balance. Extend these account balances to the debit column of the balance sheet section of the worksheet. Any asset account that is not affected by an adjustment will be transferred to the balance sheet section in the same manner.

Extend the asset Supplies. The Supplies account has a trial balance debit of $4,319.00. However, to bring this account up-to-date, an adjustment of $1,341.00 was made. Therefore, when extending Supplies on the worksheet, the trial balance debit amount of $4,319.00 is *decreased by a credit* of $1,341.00 in the adjustments section which results in an extended amount in the balance sheet debit column of $2,978.00.

Extend the asset Prepaid Insurance. The Prepaid Insurance account has a trial balance debit of $1,600.00. However, to bring this account up to date an adjustment of $330.00 was made. Therefore, when extending Prepaid Insurance on the worksheet, the trial balance debit of $1,600.00 is *decreased by a credit* of $330.00 in the adjustments section which results in an extended amount in the balance sheet debit column of $1,270.00.

2. **Extend the liability account balances.** Credit balances for all liabilities are extended to the credit column of the balance sheet section. As the extension is made, check that the balance is the up-to-date balance and has not been changed by an adjustment.

3. **Extend the owner's equity account balances.** The credit balance of the owner's capital is extended to the credit column of the balance sheet section. Verify that the transfer is an up-to-date extension not affected by an adjustment. The debit balance of the owner's drawing account is extended to the debit column of the balance sheet Section. Check that the balance was not changed by an adjustment.

Lawson's Lawn Care
Worksheet
For the Month Ended July 31, 20—

ACCOUNT TITLE	TRIAL BALANCE DEBIT	TRIAL BALANCE CREDIT	ADJUSTMENTS DEBIT	ADJUSTMENTS CREDIT	INCOME STATEMENT DEBIT	INCOME STATEMENT CREDIT	BALANCE SHEET DEBIT	BALANCE SHEET CREDIT
Cash	7822 00						7822 00	
Petty Cash	300 00						300 00	
Supplies	4319 00			(a)1341 00			2978 00	
Prepaid Insurance	1600 00			(b) 330 00			1270 00	
John's Garage		1630 00						1630 00
Wick Supplies		300 00						300 00
D. Lawson, Capital		9000 00						9000 00
D. Lawson, Drawing	500 00						500 00	
Sales		4367 00				**1** 4367 00		
Advertising Expense	86 00				**2** 86 00			
Insurance Expense			(b) 330 00		330 00			
Miscellaneous Expense	95 00				95 00			
Rent Expense	450 00				450 00			
Supplies Expense			(a)1341 00		1341 00			
Utilities Expense	125 00				125 00			
Totals	15297 00	15297 00	1671 00	1671 00	**3** 2427 00	4367 00	12870 00	10930 00
Net Income					**4** 1940 00			**4** 1940 00
					5 4367 00	4367 00	12870 00	12870 00

The Income Statement Section

This section contains the balances of all revenue and expense accounts. Revenue and expense accounts follow the assets, liabilities and owner's equity accounts on the trial balance. Their balances are extended after completing the balance sheet section of the worksheet.

1. **Extend the revenue account balance.** Always check the adjustments column to make sure that these account balances are not changed. The revenue account, Sales, has a credit balance of $4,367.00 in the trial balance credit column. This amount is extended to the credit column of the income statement section of the worksheet.

2. **Extend the balances of all expenses.** Always check the adjustment column to make sure that these account balances are not changed. All expenses without adjustments are extended in the same way.

The balance of Insurance Expense in the trial balance debit column is zero. However, there was an adjustment made to bring this account up to date. The account balance must be changed by extending the Insurance Expense adjustment debit amount of $330.00 to the income statement debit column for Insurance Expense.

The balance of Supplies Expense in the trial balance debit column is zero. However, there was an adjustment made to bring this account up to date. The account balance must be changed by extending the Supplies Expense adjustment debit amount of $1,341.00 to the income statement debit column for Supplies Expense.

Any adjusted expense account balance is extended in the same way.

Calculating Net Income

The net income is the difference between total revenue and total expenses when total revenue is greater than total expenses. The income statement section includes both the revenue and expense for the fiscal period. After the columns have been totaled, the total expenses (the debit column total) are subtracted from total revenue (the credit column total) to find the net income.

3. **Rule a single line across the remaining four columns of the worksheet.** Add the debit and credit columns and enter the total on the next line below.

4. **Calculate the Net Income** by subtracting the income statement debit total from the income statement credit total. If total revenue is greater than total expenses, the difference is the net income for the fiscal period. *Net income increases the owner's capital account* and is thus extended as a credit to the balance sheet section.

5. **Double rule the totals** to indicate that they are correct and in balance.

Calculating Net Loss

Net loss is the difference between total expenses and total revenue when total expenses are greater. The income statement section includes both the revenue and expenses for the fiscal period. After the columns have been totaled, the total revenue (the credit column total) is subtracted from total expenses (the debit column total) to find the net loss.

The net loss must also be transferred to the balance sheet section of the worksheet. If total expenses are greater than total revenue, the difference is the net loss for the fiscal period. *Net loss decreases the owner's capital account* and is thus extended as a debit to the balance sheet section. See the example below:

Totals	15297 00	15297 00	4248 00	4248 00	5004 00	4367 00	10293 00	10930 00
Net Loss						637 00	637 00	
					5004 00	5004 00	10930 00	10930 00

30

Finding and Correcting Errors

Errors may not be discovered until the end-of-the-period work is started. Items not posted may not show up until the worksheet trial balance columns do not equal. Another type of error will occur when the balances from the general ledger are not copied correctly to the worksheet. Errors can also be made on the worksheet like adding incorrectly, making improper adjustments and extending amounts incorrectly.

Any errors discovered during the preparation of the worksheet or on the worksheet itself must be corrected before proceeding with the completion of the worksheet or any financial statements. That's why worksheets (and only worksheets) are completed in pencil.

Checking for Errors on the Worksheet. When the trial balance columns for a worksheet are not in balance, find the difference between the columns then follow the guidelines listed below:

1. **The difference is 1** (that is, $.01, $.10, $1.00, or $10.00). The error is most likely in addition. Add the columns again.
2. **The difference can be divided evenly by 2.** For example, the difference is $40.00. The $40.00 ÷ 2 = $20. This usually indicates that an amount was entered in the wrong column. Look for the $20.00 that was recorded as a debit and should have been recorded as a credit or the $20.00 credit that should have been a debit.

31

3. **The difference can be divided evenly by 9.** For example, the difference is $27.00. This difference of $27 ÷ 9 equal $3.00. Remember, the result must equal a number and have no remainder. This indicates that a number may have been transposed. The $27.00 should have been $72.00. It also could determine the error was a slide. A slide occurs when a number is moved one place to the right or left. For example $150.00 is written as $15.00 or $12.00 is written as $120.00.

4. **The difference is an amount that was omitted.** For example, the difference is $25.00. Look for an account with a balance of $25.00. This balance may not have been entered on the worksheet. It may not have been copied correctly. It may be in the wrong column. Any $50.00 handled incorrectly will force the trial balance out of balance.

Additional Steps for Worksheet Errors.

1. **Trial Balance Column Errors:**
   - Make sure that all the general ledger account balances have been copied correctly.
   - Make sure that all the general ledger account balances have been recorded in the correct trial balance column.

   Solution: Correct all mistakes and add the columns again.

2. **Adjustments Column Errors:**
   - Make sure the debits and credits in the adjustments column equal. Check each debit and credit by making the small letters for each adjusted amount.
   - Check the math of each adjustment to determine that it is correct.

   Solution: Correct all errors and add the columns again.

Checking for Errors in the General Ledger. Sometimes differences between the columns on the worksheet are not related to mistakes on the worksheet but to errors that occur in the general ledger. These errors are the result of improper posting or arithmetic errors in determining the account balances. Therefore, it is important to check the accuracy of the general ledger by observing the following procedures:

1. **Verify that all amounts have been posted from all journals.**
   - If not, post all items missed and correct the balance.
   - Record the new balance on the worksheet.

2. **Make sure all the amounts have been posted to the correct accounts.**
   - If not, draw a line through the incorrect entry.
   - Determine the new balance of the account, then correct the balance on the worksheet.
   - Enter the amount in the proper account and recalculate the balance.
   - Enter the new balance on the worksheet. NOTE: Since journal and ledger entries are permanent records, *never erase a number*. Always draw a line through the entry or number and write the correct amount above it. Erasures may be made on the worksheet, however.

3. **Verify that all the dollar amounts are written correctly.**
   - Make sure that all the dollar amounts are posted to the debit or credit column of an account.
   - If an amount has been incorrectly written, draw a line through the amount and write the correct amount above it.

Account Title: *Supplies Expense*					Account No. *550*			
Date 20—	Explanation	Post. Ref.	Debit	Credit	Balance			
					Debit		Credit	
Apr 12		G1	~~693~~ 639	00 00	~~693~~ 639	00 00		

Errors That May Not Show on a Trial Balance

1. A complete transaction entered twice.
2. A transaction that was never journalized.
3. A debit part of a transaction posted as a debit to the wrong account.
4. An amount journalized incorrectly.

The easiest way to prevent errors is to work carefully, checking the work at each step in the accounting procedure. Most errors are caused by careless arithmetic. If an error is discovered, correct it before proceeding with the accounting process.

Review of Worksheet Procedures

1. Prepare the worksheet heading: *Who* (business name), *What* (worksheet) and *When* (period of time covered by worksheet).
2. Copy the account balances from the General Ledger to the trial balance columns of the worksheet.
3. Total the trial balance. The equality of debits and credits in the general ledger must be proven.
4. Plan the adjustments needed for this fiscal period. Assets such as supplies and insurance are expended during the fiscal period but their account balances do not reflect the actual inventory at the end of the fiscal period. Therefore, it is necessary to adjust these accounts to bring them up to date. The adjusting entries are made in the adjustments columns of the worksheet to accomplish this.
5. Prove the equality of the adjustments column.
6. Extend the assets, liabilities, owner's equity and owner's drawing to the balance sheet section of the worksheet. Remember to adjust the balance of the accounts affected by the entries in the adjustments columns of the worksheet.
7. Extend the revenue and expenses to the income statement section of the worksheet. Remember to carry the adjusted amounts to the proper columns.
8. Determine the net income or net loss.
9. Total and rule the worksheet.

Summary

1. The first step in preparing a worksheet is to complete the heading. The heading consists of the name of the business, the name of the working paper and the date covered by the working paper.

who what when

2. A worksheet is prepared at the end of every fiscal period.

1 mon. quarterly six mon. 1 yr.

3. A worksheet is completed to determine the need for and to make any necessary adjustment to bring accounts up to date, to separate all accounts into the proper financial statement and to check the accuracy of all mathematical calculations.

4. The trial balance is prepared from the balance of the accounts in the general ledger.

5. The equality of the trial balance totals proves the accuracy of the posting and balancing of all general ledger accounts.

6. The adjustment columns of the worksheet are used to bring the balances of certain asset accounts up to date.

7. The assets, liabilities, owner's equity and owner's drawing accounts are copied to the balance sheet section of the worksheet.

8. The revenue and expense accounts are transferred to the income statement section of the worksheet.

9. The net income or net loss is determined by finding the difference between the subtotals of the income statement debit and credit columns.

10. A net income exists when the revenue (income statement credit column) is larger than the Expenses (income statement debit column).

11. A net loss occurs when the expenses (income statement debit column) are larger than the Revenue (income statement credit column).

12. The income statement section of the worksheet provides all the information necessary to prepare the formal financial statement known as the income statement.

13. The balance sheet section of the worksheet provides all the necessary information to prepare the formal balance sheet and the formal income statement.

14. After the completion of the worksheet, all financial statements must be prepared.

Complete the following activity.

On October 31 of the current year **Clever Closet Company** had the following general ledger accounts and balances. The business has a monthly fiscal period.

Account Titles	Debit Balance	Credit Balance
Cash	13,321.00	
Petty Cash	300.00	
Supplies	3,900.00	
Prepaid Insurance	1,200.00	
Tyson Office Supply		1,166.00
Office Systems, Inc.		960.00
Joanne Clever, Capital		15,000.00
Joanne Clever, Drawing	860.00	
Sales		3,675.00
Advertising Expense	175.00	
Insurance Expense		
Miscellaneous Expense	85.00	
Rent Expense	550.00	
Repair Expense	285.00	
Supplies Expense		
Utilities Expense	125.00	

Instructions:

2.1   a. Prepare the heading on the worksheet.

     b. Prepare the trial balance. Enter account titles and balances.

     c. Total and rule the trial balance columns.

     d. Analyze the following adjustment information into debit and credit parts. Record the adjustments on the worksheet adjustments columns.

Value of Supplies on Hand: $2,200.00

Value of Prepaid Insurance: $900.00

     e. Total and rule the adjustments columns.

     f. Extend the updated balances to the balance sheet columns.

     g. Extend the updated balances to the income statement columns.

     h. Rule a single line across the income statement and balance sheet columns. Total the columns. Calculate the net income or net loss. Label the amount properly in the account title column.

     i. Total and rule the income statement and balance sheet columns.

Clever Closet Company
Worksheet
For the month ended October 31, 2000

ACCOUNT NAME	TRIAL BALANCE DEBIT	TRIAL BALANCE CREDIT	ADJUSTMENTS DEBIT	ADJUSTMENTS CREDIT	INCOME STATEMENT DEBIT	INCOME STATEMENT CREDIT	BALANCE SHEET DEBIT	BALANCE SHEET CREDIT
Cash	13,321 00						13,321 00	
Petty cash	300 00						300 00	
Supplies	3,900 00			ᵃ 1700 00			2200 00	
Prepaid insurance	1,200 00			ᵇ 300 00			900 00	
Tyson Office Supply		1100 00						1100 00
Office System, Inc.		960 00						960 00
Joanne Clever, Capital		15,000 00						15,000 00
Joanne Clever, Drawing	860 00						860 00	
Sales		3,675 00				3,675 00		
Advertising Expense	175 00				175 00			
Insurance Expense			ᵇ 300 00		300 00			
Miscellaneous Expense	85 00				85 00			
Rent Expense	550 00				550 00			
Repair Expense	285 00				285 00			
Supplies Expense			ᵃ 1700 00		1700 00			
Utility Expense	125 00				125 00			
Total	20,801 00	20,801 00	2000 00	2000 00	3220 00	3,675 00	17,581 00	17,126 00
Net Income					455 00			455 00
					3,675 00	3,675 00	17,581 00	17,581 00

36

Review the material in this section in preparation for the Self Test. This Self Test will check your mastery of this particular section as well as your knowledge of the previous section.

SELF TEST 2

Match the following accounting terms with their definitions (each answer, 2 points).

2.01 __i__   a proof of the equality of debits and credits in a general ledger

2.02 __M__   indicates the totals are correct and in balance

2.03 __F__   occurs when total revenue is greater than total expenses

2.04 __l__   indicates the entries are complete above and are totaled below

2.05 __D__   the length of the accounting cycle for which a business summarizes and reports financial information

2.06 __E__   a financial statement that reports the revenue and expenses for a fiscal period

2.07 __G__   occurs when total expenses are greater than total revenue

2.08 __H__   drawing a line

2.09 __C__   the same accounting concepts are applied the same way for each accounting period for as long as the business operates

2.010 __B__   a financial statement that reports assets, liabilities and owner's equity on a specific date

2.011 __J__   informal, informational papers provided by accountants to owners and manager

2.012 __K__   a columnar accounting form used to summarize the general ledger information needed to prepare financial statements

2.013 __A__   an amount that is added to or subtracted from an account balance to bring the balance up to date

a. adjustment

b. balance sheet

c. consistent reporting

d. fiscal period

e. income statement

f. net income

g. net loss

h. ruling

i. trial balance

j. working papers

k. worksheet

l. single line

m. double line

n. posting

o. journalizing

37

Complete the following activities (each answer, 5 points).

2.014   List four reasons for preparing a worksheet.

FROM The Ledger.

a. ~~PRepares~~ The unadjusted Trail balance to prove The equality of The debit & credit balance taken

b. Shows The EFFects of The adjustments on THE account balance to bring them up to INCOME STATEMENTS or account balances

c. Sorts The account balances into columns desiding whether the accounts are for PREParing

d. Calulates the Net income & NET loss FOR The fiscal PERioD.

2.015   Why are accounting records completed in ink? *The accounTING RECORDS are complet IN INK so They cannot be changed with/o being NoTiced. They are permanente records & People aren'T suppost to mess with the Numbers. People can steal that way. Thats why they're do IN INK*

Complete this activity (50 points total).

2.016   Use the worksheet on the next page to complete these activities:

  a.   Prove (rule and total) the trial balance section (4 points).

  b.   Make the following adjustments and prove the adjustments section (12 points):

   • The ending inventory for supplies was $3,311.00. Calculate total supplies used during the fiscal period and use that amount to make the adjusting entry in the worksheet.

   • The value of the unused Prepaid Insurance at the end of the fiscal period was $1,450.00.

  c.   Extend the permanent account balances to the correct columns in the balance sheet section of the worksheet (9 points).

  d.   Extend the revenue and expense account balances to the correct columns in the income statement section of the worksheet (7 points).

  e.   Rule and total the last four columns, then calculate net income or net loss and complete the worksheet (18 points).

81 / 101

Score _____

Adult Check _____

Initial   Date

Worksheet for Self Test Exercise 2.016

Lawson's Lawn Service
Worksheet
For the Month Ended July 31, 20—

ACCOUNT NAME	TRIAL BALANCE DEBIT	TRIAL BALANCE CREDIT	ADJUSTMENTS DEBIT	ADJUSTMENTS CREDIT	INCOME STATEMENT DEBIT	INCOME STATEMENT CREDIT	BALANCE SHEET DEBIT	BALANCE SHEET CREDIT
Cash	7822 00						7822 00	
Petty Cash	300 00						300 00	
Supplies	4319 00			(a) 1008 00			3311 00	
Prepaid Insurance	1600 00			(b) 150 00			1450 00	
John's Garage		1630 00						1630 00
Wick Supplies		300 00						300 00
Donald Lawson, Capital		9000 00						9000 00
Donald Lawson, Drawing	500 00						500	
Sales		4367 00				4367 00		
Advertising Expense	86 00				86 00			
Insurance Expense			(b) 150 00		150 00			
Miscellaneous Expense	95 00				95 00			
Rent Expense	450 00				450 00			
Supplies Expense			(a) 1008 00		1008 00			
Utilities Expense	125 00				135 00			
Total	15,397 00	15,397 00	1158 00	1158 00	1914 60	4367 00	13,383 00	16,930 00
NET INCOME					2453 00			2453 00
					4367 00	4367 00	13,383 00	13,383 00

SECTION III. REVIEW & APPLICATION PROBLEMS

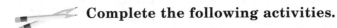 **Complete the following activities.**

Preparing a Formal Trial Balance:

3.1   From the list of account titles and balances below, prepare a formal trial balance for **Lawrence Landscaping** for the month ended January 31 of the current year. NOTE: Be sure to enter the accounts and their balances in the proper sequence.

Account Title	Account No.	Debit Balance	Credit Balance
Utility Expense	550	$ 1,500.00	
Cash	110	22,000.00	
Salary Expense	540	6,000.00	
Jay Lawrence, Capital	310		22,650.00
Supplies	130	2,500.00	
Jones Company	210		5,715.00
Jay Lawrence, Drawing	320	850.00	
Advertising Expense	510	9,950.00	
Sales	410		28,500.00
Prepaid Insurance	140	1,600.00	
Rent Expense	530	12,000.00	
Petty Cash	120	300.00	
Miscellaneous Expense	520	165.00	

Lawrence Landscaping
Trial Balance
~~F~~ ED JANUARY 31, 2002

ACCOUNT TITLE	ACCT. NO.	DEBIT	CREDIT
Cash	110	22,000 00	
Petty Cash	120	300 00	
Supplies	130	2,500 00	
Prepaid Insurance	140	1,600 00	
Jones Company	210		5,715 00
Jay Lawrence, Capital	310		22,650 00
Jay Lawrence, Drawing	320	850 00	
Sales	410		28,500 00
Advertising Expense	510	9,950 00	
Miscellaneous Expense	520	165 00	
Rent Expense	530	12,000 00	
Salary Expense	540	6,000 00	
Utility Expense	550	1,500 00	
Totals		56,865 00	56,865 00

40

Extending Account Balances on a Worksheet:

3.2   Place a check mark (✔) in each column of the six-column worksheet below where the balances of the following accounts will appear.

ACCOUNT TITLE	TRIAL BALANCE		INCOME STATEMENT		BALANCE SHEET	
	Debit	Credit	Debit	Credit	Debit	Credit
Cash	✓					
Miscellaneous Expense	✓		✓			
Office Max		✓				✓
M. Johnson, Capital		✓				✓
Sales		✓		✓		
Office Supplies	✓				✓	
Utility Expense	✓		✓			
Insurance Expense	✓		✓			
Petty Cash	✓				✓	
Rent Expense	✓		✓			
M. Johnson, Drawing	✓				✓	✗
Prepaid Insurance	✓				✓	
Store Supplies	✓				✓	
Notes Payable		✓				✓

Complete this activity.

George Smith wanted to complete a worksheet from his ledger accounts. He recorded the names of the accounts and the account balances on the trial balance columns of a worksheet. However, the trial balance did not balance.

3.3 Total the original trial balance columns to find out the difference, then find the error and redo the trial balance. NOTE: for ease in completing the corrected trial balance, the ledger accounts show balances only.

Smith's Septic Service
Worksheet
For the Month Ended November 30, 20—

ACCOUNT TITLE	ORIGINAL TRIAL BALANCE			CORRECTED TRIAL BALANCE	
	DEBIT	CREDIT		DEBIT	CREDIT
Cash	3700 00			3700 00	
Supplies	950 00			950 00	
Prepaid Insurance	450 00			450 00	
Wooten's Chemicals		550 00			550 00
Joe's Trucking		650 00			650 00
G. Smith, Capital		3880 00			3880 00
G. Smith, Drawing	350 00			350 00	
Sales		1250 00			1250 00
Advertising Expense	305 00			350 00	
Insurance Expense					
Miscellaneous Expense	80 00			80 00	
Rent Expense	450 00			450 00	
Supplies Expense					
Totals	6,285 00	6330 00		6330 00	6330 00

6285   6330

diff. 45

Account Title: *Cash*						Account No. *110*	
Date 20—	Explanation	Post. Ref.	Debit	Credit	Balance		
					Debit	Credit	
Nov. 30			3,700 00		3700 00		

42

Account Title: Supplies   **Account No.** 120

Date 20—	Explanation	Post. Ref.	Debit	Credit	Balance Debit	Balance Credit
Nov. 30			950 00		950 00	

Account Title: Prepaid Insurance   **Account No.** 130

Date 20—	Explanation	Post. Ref.	Debit	Credit	Balance Debit	Balance Credit
Nov. 30			450 00		450 00	

Account Title: Wooten's Chemicals   **Account No.** 210

Date 20—	Explanation	Post. Ref.	Debit	Credit	Balance Debit	Balance Credit
Nov. 30			550 00			550 00

Account Title: Joe's Trucking   **Account No.** 220

Date 20—	Explanation	Post. Ref.	Debit	Credit	Balance Debit	Balance Credit
Nov. 30			650 00			650 00

Account Title: George Smith, Capital   **Account No.** 310

Date 20—	Explanation	Post. Ref.	Debit	Credit	Balance Debit	Balance Credit
Nov. 30			3880 00			3880 00

Account Title: George Smith, Drawing   Account No. 320

Date 20—	Explanation	Post. Ref.	Debit	Credit	Balance Debit	Balance Credit
Nov. 30			350 00		350 00	

Account Title: Sales   Account No. 410

Date 20—	Explanation	Post. Ref.	Debit	Credit	Balance Debit	Balance Credit
Nov. 30				1250 00		1250 00

Account Title: Advertising Expense   Account No. 510

Date 20—	Explanation	Post. Ref.	Debit	Credit	Balance Debit	Balance Credit
Nov. 30			305 00		350 00	

Account Title: Insurance Expense   Account No. 520

Date 20—	Explanation	Post. Ref.	Debit	Credit	Balance Debit	Balance Credit
Nov. 30						

Account Title: Miscellaneous Expense   Account No. 530

Date 20—	Explanation	Post. Ref.	Debit	Credit	Balance Debit	Balance Credit
Nov. 30			80		80 00	

Account Title: *Rent Expense*					Account No. *540*			
Date 20—	**Explanation**	**Post. Ref.**	**Debit**	**Credit**	**Balance**			
					Debit		**Credit**	
Nov. 30			450 00		450 00			

Account Title: *Supplies Expense*					Account No. *550*			
Date 20—	**Explanation**	**Post. Ref.**	**Debit**	**Credit**	**Balance**			
					Debit		**Credit**	
Nov. 30								

 Complete this activity.

3.4   The trial balance may be in balance even if errors have been made. From the statements below, circle *YES* if the trial balance will be in balance or *NO* if it will not be in balance if the error is made.

a.   A complete transaction (debit part and credit part) was journalized more than once.   (YES)   NO

b.   A transaction was posted as follows: the debit was posted as 50 and the credit was posted as 5.   YES   (NO)

c.   A transaction was journalized and never posted.   (YES)   ~~NO~~

d.   A transaction was never entered in any journal.   (YES)   NO

e.   An amount charged to Advertising Expense was accidentally posted to Miscellaneous Expense.   (YES)   NO

f.   An amount was recorded incorrectly from the source document and was then posted as the incorrect amount.   (YES)   NO

45

Complete the following activity.

On November 30 of the current year, **Floor-Shine Company** has the following general ledger accounts and balances. The business has a **monthly** fiscal period.

Account Titles	Debit Balance	Credit Balance
Cash	5,844.00	
Petty Cash	300.00	
Supplies	1,900.00	
Prepaid Insurance	800.00	
Tyson Office Supply		166.00
Office Systems, Inc.		60.00
Mike Ford, Capital		8,000.00
Mike Ford, Drawing	560.00	
Sales		1,628.00
Advertising Expense	75.00	
Insurance Expense		
Miscellaneous Expense	15.00	
Rent Expense	250.00	
Repair Expense	85.00	
Supplies Expense		
Utilities Expense	25.00	

Instructions:

3.5

a. Prepare the heading on the worksheet.

b. Prepare the trial balance. Enter account titles and balances.

c. Total and rule the trial balance columns.

d. Analyze the following adjustment information into debit and credit parts. Record the adjustments on the worksheet adjustments columns.

> Value of Supplies on Hand: $1,300.00
>
> Value of Prepaid Insurance: $400.00

e. Total and rule the adjustments columns.

f. Extend the updated balances to the balance sheet columns.

g. Extend the updated balances to the income statement columns.

h. Rule a single line across the income statement and balance sheet columns. Total the columns. Calculate the net income or net loss. Label the amount properly in the account title column.

i. Total and rule the income statement and balance sheet columns.

Worksheet for Exercise 3.5

Floor-Shine Company
Worksheet
For the month ended November 30, 2002

ACCOUNT NAME	TRIAL BALANCE DEBIT	TRIAL BALANCE CREDIT	ADJUSTMENTS DEBIT	ADJUSTMENTS CREDIT	INCOME STATEMENT DEBIT	INCOME STATEMENT CREDIT	BALANCE SHEET DEBIT	BALANCE SHEET CREDIT
Cash	5,844 00						5844 00	
Petty Cash	300 00						300 00	
Supplies	1900 00			(a)600 00			1300 00	
Prepaid Insurance	800 00			(b)400 00			400 00	
Tyson Office Supply		166 00						166 00
Office Systems, Inc.		60 00						60 00
Mike Ford, Capital		9,000 00						9,000 00
Mike Ford Drawing	500 00						500 00	
Sales		1,628 00				1628 00		
Advertising Expense	75 00				75 00			
Insurance Expense			(b)400 00		400 00			
Miscellaneous Expense	15 00				15 00			
Rent Expense	250 00				250 00			
Repairs Expense	85 00				85 00			
Supplies Expense			(a)600 00		600 00			
Utilities Expense	25 00				25 00			
Total	9,854 00	9854 00	1000 00	1000 00	1450 00	1628 00	8404 00	8226 00
Net Income					178 00			178 00
					1628 00	1628 00	8404 00	8404 00

Complete this activity.

On March 31 of the current year, **Fox Photography** has the following general ledger accounts and balances. The business has a **quarterly** fiscal period.

Account Titles	Debit Balance	Credit Balance
Cash	10,454.00	
Petty Cash	300.00	
Supplies – Office	2,950.00	
Supplies – Store	1,895.00	
Prepaid Insurance	3,800.00	
Jones Office Supply		3,666.00
Maines Supply, Inc.		1,660.00
Mike Fox, Capital		12,585.00
Mike Fox, Drawing	1,560.00	
Sales		8,628.00
Advertising Expense	2,775.00	
Insurance Expense		
Miscellaneous Expense	615.00	
Rent Expense	1,280.00	
Repair Expense	885.00	
Supplies Expense – Office		
Supplies Expense – Store		
Utilities Expense	25.00	

Instructions:

3.6

a. Prepare the heading on the worksheet.

b. Prepare the trial balance. Enter account titles and balances.

c. Total and rule the trial balance columns.

d. Analyze the following adjustment information into debit and credit parts. Record the adjustments on the worksheet adjustments columns.

> Value of Office Supplies on Hand: $1,101.00
>
> Value of Store Supplies on Hand: $895.00
>
> Value of Prepaid Insurance: $2,400.00

e. Total and rule the adjustments columns.

f. Extend the updated balances to the balance sheet columns.

g. Extend the updated balances to the income statement columns.

h. Rule a single line across the income statement and balance sheet columns. Total the columns. Calculate the net income or net loss. Label the amount properly in the account title column.

i. Total and rule the income statement and balance sheet columns.

Worksheet for Exercise 3.6

Fox Photography
Worksheet
For month ended March 31, 20—

ACCOUNT NAME	TRIAL BALANCE DEBIT	TRIAL BALANCE CREDIT	ADJUSTMENTS DEBIT	ADJUSTMENTS CREDIT	INCOME STATEMENT DEBIT	INCOME STATEMENT CREDIT	BALANCE SHEET DEBIT	BALANCE SHEET CREDIT
Cash	10,454.00						10,454.00	
Petty Cash	300.00						300.00	
Supplies – Office	2950.00			(a)1849.00			1,101.00	
Supplies – Stores	1895.00			(b)1000.00			895.00	
Prepaid Insurance	3800.00			(c)1400.00			2,400.00	
Jones Office Supply		3,666.00						3,666.00
Morris Supply, Inc.		1,660.00						1,660.00
Mike Fox, Capital		12,585.00						12,585.00
Mike Fox, Drawing	1560.00						1,560.00	
Sales		8628.00				8628.00		
Advertising Expense	2775.00				2775.00			
Insurance Expense			(c)1400.00		1400.00			
Miscellaneous Expense	615.00				615.00			
Rent Expense	1280.00				1280.00			
Repair Expense	885.00				885.00			
Supplies Expense – Office			(a)1849.00		1849.00			
Supplies Expense – Stores			(b)1000.00		1000.00			
Utilities Expense	25.00				25.00			
Total	26,539.00	26,539.00	4249.00	4249.00	9829.00	8628.00	16,710.00	17,911.00
Net Income						1201.00	1201.00	
					9829.00	9829.00	17,911.00	17,911.00

Ashley C. Ashley C Elizabeth Bird

49

Complete this activity.

On May 31 of the current year, **Bob's Boat Rental** has the following general ledger accounts and balances. The business has a **quarterly** fiscal period.

Account Titles	Debit Balance	Credit Balance
Cash	18,556.00	
Petty Cash	450.00	
Supplies – Office	1,950.00	
Supplies – Store	2,694.00	
Prepaid Insurance	6,400.00	
Blue Heaven Marine		2,981.00
Lake View Supply, Inc.		1,537.00
Robert Borden, Capital		18,688.00
Robert Borden, Drawing	2,590.00	
Boat Rental		16,548.00
Fishing Equipment Sales		18,301.00
Advertising Expense	12,165.00	
Insurance Expense		
Miscellaneous Expense	2,158.00	
Rent Expense	6,000.00	
Repair Expense	2,603.00	
Supplies Expense – Office		
Supplies Expense – Store		
Utilities Expense	2,489.00	

Instructions:

3.7

a. Prepare the heading on the worksheet.

b. Prepare the trial balance. Enter account titles and balances.

c. Total and rule the trial balance columns.

d. Analyze the following adjustment information into debit and credit parts. Record the adjustments on the worksheet adjustments columns.

> Value of Office Supplies on hand: $1,208.00
>
> Value of Store Supplies on hand: $1,408.00
>
> Value of Prepaid Insurance: $5,530.00

e. Total and rule the adjustments columns.

f. Extend the updated balances to the balance sheet columns.

g. Extend the updated balances to the income statement columns.

h. Rule a single line across the income statement and balance sheet columns. Total the columns. Calculate the net income or net loss. Label the amount properly in the account title column.

i. Total and rule the income statement and balance sheet columns.

Worksheet for Exercise 3.7

Bob's Boat Rental
Worksheet
For Month ended May 31, 2009

ACCOUNT NAME	TRIAL BALANCE		ADJUSTMENTS		INCOME STATEMENT		BALANCE SHEET	
	DEBIT	CREDIT	DEBIT	CREDIT	DEBIT	CREDIT	DEBIT	CREDIT
Cash	18,556 00						18,556 00	
Petty Cash	450 00						450 00	
Supplies - Office	1950 00			(a) 742 00			1208 00	
Supplies - Store	2,694 00			(b) 1286 00			1408 00	
Prepaid Insurance	6,400 00			(c) 870 00			5,530 00	
Blue Heaven Marine		2981 00						2981 00
Lake View Supply, Inc.		1537 00						1537 00
Robert Borden, Capital		18,688 00						18,688 00
Robert Borden, Drawing	2500 00						2500 00	
Boat Rental		16,548 00				16,548 00		
Fishing Equipment Sales		18,301 00				18,301 00		
Advertising Expense	12,165 00				12,165 00			
Insurance Expense			(c) 870 00		870 00			
Miscellaneous Expense	3,158 00				3,158 00			
Rent Expense	6,000 00				6,000 00			
Repair Expense	2,003 00				2,003 00			
Supplies Expense - Office			(a) 742 00		742 00			
Supplies Expense - Store			(b) 1286 00		1286 00			
Utilities Expense	3489 00				3489 00			
Total	58,055 00	58,055 00	2898 00	2898 00	28,813 00	34,849 00	29,746 00	23,806 00
Net Income					6,536 00			1,536 00
					34,849 00	34,849 00		

2 31 2 3

51

Complete this activity.

On September 30 of the current year, **Donald Frost, M.D.** has the following general ledger accounts and balances. The business has a **quarterly** fiscal period.

Account Titles	Debit Balance	Credit Balance
Cash	38,958.00	
Petty Cash	300.00	
Supplies – Office	4,982.00	
Supplies – Medical	5,287.00	
Prepaid Insurance	4,800.00	
Adams Office Supply		13,600.00
Johnson & Johnson, Inc.		9,773.00
Donald Frost, Capital		23,514.00
Donald Frost, Drawing	8,560.00	
Office Fees Revenue		28,650.00
Prescription Revenue		14,982.00
Advertising Expense	6,775.00	
Insurance Expense		
Miscellaneous Expense	1,615.00	
Rent Expense	12,450.00	
Repair Expense	2,897.00	
Supplies Expense – Office		
Supplies Expense – Medical		
Utilities Expense	3,895.00	

Instructions:

3.8
a. Prepare the heading on the worksheet.

b. Prepare the trial balance. Enter account titles and balances.

c. Total and rule the trial balance columns.

d. Analyze the following adjustment information into debit and credit parts. Record the adjustments on the worksheet adjustments columns.

Value of Office Supplies on hand: $1,100.00

Value of Medical Supplies on hand: $2,992.00

Value of Prepaid Insurance: $3,600.00

e. Total and rule the adjustments columns.

f. Extend the updated balances to the balance sheet columns.

g. Extend the updated balances to the income statement columns.

h. Rule a single line across the income statement and balance sheet columns. Total the columns. Calculate the net income or net loss. Label the amount properly in the account title column.

i. Total and rule the income statement and balance sheet columns.

Worksheet for Exercise 3.8

Donald Frost, M.D.
Worksheet
For month ended September 30

ACCOUNT NAME	TRIAL BALANCE DEBIT	TRIAL BALANCE CREDIT	ADJUSTMENTS DEBIT	ADJUSTMENTS CREDIT	INCOME STATEMENT DEBIT	INCOME STATEMENT CREDIT	BALANCE SHEET DEBIT	BALANCE SHEET CREDIT
Cash	38,918 00						38,918 00	
Petty Cash	300 00						300 00	
Supplies – Office	4,982 00			(a) 3,882 00			1,100 00	
Supplies – Medical	5,287 00			(b) 2,395 00			2,892 00	
Prepaid Insurance	4,800 00			(c) 1,200 00			3,600 00	
Adams office Supply		13,600 00						13,600 00
Johnson & Johnson Inc.		9,773 00						9,773 00
Donald Frost, Capital		23,514 00						23,514 00
Donald Frost, Drawing	8,560 00						8,560 00	
Office Fees Revenue		28,650 00				28,650 00		
Prescription Revenue		14,982 00				14,982 00		
Advertising Expense	6,775 00				6,775 00			
Insurance Expense			(c) 1,200 00		1,200 00			
Miscellaneous Expense	1,615 00				1,615 00			
Rent Expense	13,450 00				13,450 00			
Repairs Expense	2,897 00				2,897 00			
Supplies – office			(a) 3,882 00		3,882 00			
Supplies – Medical Expense			(b) 2,395 00		2,395 00			
Utilities Expense	3,895 00				3,895 00			
Total	90,519 00	90,519 00	7,477 00	7,477 00	35,109 00	43,632 00	55,510 00	46,887 00
Net Income					8,623 00			8,623 00
					43,632 00	43,632 00	55,510 00	55,510 00

53

Extra 8-Column Worksheet

ACCOUNT NAME	TRIAL BALANCE		ADJUSTMENTS		INCOME STATEMENT		BALANCE SHEET	
	DEBIT	CREDIT	DEBIT	CREDIT	DEBIT	CREDIT	DEBIT	CREDIT